Buckaroo Beau
~Lives on a Ranch~

Written by
Kacy Burke

Art by
Mel Schroeder

Visit www.BuckarooBeau.com for updates or to purchase more books in this series.

For Beau
(Like everything else)

Baby Beau is a real buckaroo.

His mom and dad are buckaroos, too.

He lives on a ranch
with horses and cows.

He'll be in
charge soon,

but he just
helps for now.

He starts each day early
when the loud rooster crows.

He feeds all the
animals in the heat

and the snow.

He brushes
his horse

and throws
on his saddle,

then rides through the ranch
to herd all the cattle.

He doctors
the calves

and checks
all the fence,

and solves any problems
the day may present.

He cleans
out the stalls

and puts out
the hay

for the horses to eat
at the end of the day.

He locks up the barn
and heads home to eat,

then changes
his clothes

and props up
his feet.

After a long day of work with mom and dad,

Buckaroo Beau is ready for bed.

UNTIL NEXT TIME...

www.BuckarooBeau.com

Made in United States
Orlando, FL
01 September 2024